You're already okay

This edition first published 2018

© Marie Arymar, Realisation Works

www.realisationworks.com

Email: marie@realisationworks.com

ISBN: 978-1-78926-801-0

Printed by Exe Valley Design & Print Ltd, Exeter, Devon, UK. For more
information about Exe Valley Design & Print, please visit
www.exeprint.co.uk

The right of Marie Arymar to be identified as the Author of the Work
has been asserted by her in accordance with the Copyright, Designs and
Patents Act 1988.

Thank you to Syd Banks, Ann Ross and Rudi Kennard for your teaching and guidance both before and during this book's journey. Also huge thanks to The Figlet (aka Amelie) and Toby for being the first proof readers and providing feedback from the younger person's view point. Thank you to Kailem, Roxanne and Caroline for providing such powerful testimonies on the back page.

Thank you to Nige Sandford from Exe Valley Design & Print for his unlimited amount of time, patience and printing advice; keeping me on track every step of the way. Thank you to Jonathan Harris, who's assistance at the start helped me to see that this project was both possible and achievable. Also thanks to Tanya Rodgers for understanding what I was saying and transferring that into illustrations.

The biggest thanks of all to my husband, Jonathan Armes, who never stops believing in me.

There are times when we just haven't got a clue what's going on.

Nobody understands us.

Nobody takes time to hear us.

Our thoughts are like a massive storm in our heads; a constant thought-overload.

We can't sleep.

We snap at people.

We wish everyone saw life the way we see it – it would be so much easier that way.

MY FAULT
what should I wear to the party?
what did I do that for?
IS HE CHEATING ON ME?
I'm so Stupid
why did I say that?
what mood is she going to be in?

That's totally normal.

It's the same for every single person on the planet.

But it doesn't have to always be like this.

Not 100% of the time anyway.

What a relief if we didn't have to live like this every day.

When we understand how our mind works, we can relax a bit.

Our thoughts come through us like an energy wave.

We can't stop this energy or do anything about it.

Our thoughts just come.

It's the same energy that:

Makes the grass grow;

Ensures our hearts beat and our lungs breathe;

Makes a cow burp;

Makes a dog chase its tail.

Just like gravity keeps us fixed to the earth and stops us floating away, this principle of thought means that we will always feel exactly what we are thinking in each moment.

Just like a coin always has a head side and a tail side;

we will **always feel what we are thinking.**

They go hand in hand.

Always.

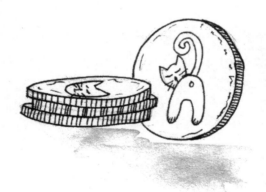

Try feeling happy when you are thinking about something really sad.

Or try feeling sad when you are thinking about something really happy.

We can't.

It just doesn't work.

That's because, just like gravity keeps us on the ground, we will always feel exactly what we are thinking in each moment.

But why can't we stop these thoughts from coming through?

We just can't.

Just like the grass keeps growing or the bees keep buzzing.

There's an energy which is bigger than us and it comes to us through passing thoughts.

What we **can** do though, is be aware that these thoughts are just passing through.

The energy of thought can *feel* powerful when it flows through us. Although thoughts often feel really real, they don't need to have power over us.

They are like clouds passing through the blue sky in our mind, so they can float in and out just as they are.

Thoughts pop in and out of our heads like popcorn!

When our thoughts about certain things start to seem really real, life might feel pretty crappy.

And out of control.

But we can just remember that these thoughts will pass and that we are already okay.

Right now — just as we are.

What we do have is a brilliant self-correcting system that points us back to who we are.

So who are we?

We are already perfect.

We are like a diamond – perfectly formed and unbreakable.

We are like the sun - always in the sky.

Even when we can't see it because of the clouds.

But the sun is still there.

The clouds always float by and we'll see the sun again.

The sun and the diamond are metaphors for who we **really** are.

Our **true** Self.

Our true or inner Self never, ever changes.

It can never be broken.

Or damaged.

It's perfect.

The voice that comes from our true Self is never wrong.

We just often choose to ignore it.

How often have we heard the inner voice say:

> I should be doing my homework;
>
> I wish I hadn't said that;
>
> That was nasty;
>
> Why won't you listen to me?

When we ignore the inner voice coming from our true Self, we start to **believe** the things that we think.

We start to **believe** the feelings that come from what we think.

It gets confusing.

Then we start to innocently believe we really are that person who is:

Bad

Wrong

A bully

Worthless

Controlling

Stupid

Not likeable

But none of it is true.

How can it be when we are perfect inside?

So when we are feeling anxious or cross or angry or unloved or confused, we can recognise that it is only our thinking in any moment.

And we can relax for just a bit.

By being aware that our thoughts don't have any *actual* power over us, we can chill out and remember that we already have everything we need to decide what to do next.

We can be a little **_kinder to ourselves._**

The thing that makes it all even more complicated is that **everyone else is going through the same stuff as us.**

So, everyone else is getting stuck in their own thought-storm.

Who does this? Everyone!

Friends

Parents

Aunts and uncles

Grandparents

Teachers

Doctors

Police officers

The person who's a bit of a bully up the road

The person who dumped you recently

The person in the local shop

Everyone

We are all getting caught up in what we are thinking about and we are all thinking different stuff.

All the time.

Other people often hide their stuff from us, just like we often hide ours from them.

So how can we possibly know what someone else is thinking?

We can't.

In that case, why do we worry so much about what **they say?**

Knowing this is the key to being kinder to **ourselves**.

When we are feeling really good, often our best friend isn't.

If we were the sea:

    Some of us would be a high tide;

    Some of us would be a low tide;

    Some of us would be a choppy sea;

    Some of us would be a calm, pond-like sea;

Then, the next day, it could all be different.

We are all in different states all the time.

Being kinder to ourselves means that we stop beating ourselves up.

We take a moment to connect back to our true Self and we know what to do next.

We don't always hear it straight away, but our inner voice will tell us the right thing to do.

Being kind to ourselves also means that we know the answer will come, so we don't need to react in our usual way.

We feel okay once we know that the other person is just caught up in their own thought-storm... and that their moment of overthinking will pass too.

This means that, actually, none of what's going on is anything to do with us.

Then we find we get into fewer arguments or we don't snap too quickly.

We start to feel a bit more resilient.

We become calmer.

People start to be drawn to us.

We know that we are okay as we are.

We are keeping our power just for us.

So what about remembering stuff from the past?

Well, that's just more thinking.

Memories are ghost thoughts.

But we can't do anything about the past.

It's over.

What's the point in giving our power to stuff that happened years ago?

Depressive thinking is a thought-storm about the past.

So what about getting worried about stuff in the future?

Well, that's more thinking.

Anxious thinking about stuff which may or may not happen in the future.

But we can't do anything about the future.

It hasn't happened yet and **no one can predict the future.**

What's the point in giving our power to stuff that may or may not **ever even happen?**

Anxious thinking is a thought-storm about the future.

So, if we are already okay - perfect like a diamond.

And the true essence of who we are can't be broken.

And we know that we are getting caught up in thought-storms.

And we know we can't change the past.

And we can't predict the future.

And we can keep the power for ourselves.

Where does this leave us?

It leaves us right here.

Right now.

In the present moment.

With the head space to take a bit of time.

To remember that we are okay.

And to listen to our Truth inside.

We can feel:

Connected

Resilient

Calm

Strong

Kind to ourselves

Kind to others

Full of love

Loved

And you know what?

The times when we don't feel this?

That's okay too.

Because we are like the tide:

   We ebb and we flow.

Because we are like the sun:

   We are sometimes covered by cloud.

But the sun is **always** shining in the sky,
even when we can't see it.

We are,

And always will be,

Perfect.

About the author

Marie Arymar has worked with young people throughout her career; as a youth worker, a youth development officer, a college lecturer and pastoral lead in three large further education colleges.

She runs Realisation Works, a company which offers well-being coaching to primarily children and young adults, either face to face or online, through small group work, or through links with organisations.

She also supports students at the University of Exeter, plus works with Young Devon, a local charity, supporting victims of crime aged 10 - 25.

Marie lives in Exeter with her family and mostly loves having fun outdoors in the stunning Devon countryside.

She really hopes you enjoyed this book, if so, please leave a review on Amazon.